To Steward and Jeni
with the author's compliment
and all good wishes
Jerry

Crail '87

BROUGHT UP TO LEAVE

Brought up to Leave

DERRY JEFFARES

COLIN SMYTHE
Gerrards Cross 1987

First published in 1987 by Colin Smythe Limited
Gerrards Cross, Buckinghamshire

British Library Cataloguing in Publication Data
Jeffares, Derry
Brought up to leave
I. Title
821'.914   PR6019.E26

ISBN 0-86140-254-5

Produced in Great Britain
Typeset by Crypticks, Leeds,
and printed and bound by Billing & Sons Ltd., Worcester

TO TAIKAN

ACKNOWLEDGEMENTS

Acknowledgements are due to the editors of the following in which some of these poems have appeared: *Ariel; Contemporary Review; Etudes Irlandaises* and *Lines Review.*

Contents

WESTER MOSS

WEXFORD

August Holidays

We knew the names of all the stations:
Avoca, Woodenbridge, Arklow, Inch,
And, at last, Gorey.
Fortune's aged Armstrong Siddeley taxi,
The dusty high-hedged road,
Three miles, then down the linch
And, at last, the sea.
No Greeks ever shouted it so loud
THE SEA! THE SEA!

Limitless Limits

Between the planks of the bridge you could see it,
Greasy sinister swirl of water against the wall;
Between the iron lattice you could see them,
Old unused fishing boats moored in a line:
Then you were over, sand softening footfall,
As you gazed in wonder at the hyaline
Stretching to Wales, or further, without limit –
All of it to be recorded in a poem, item by item,
Simply, without a plan, design or stratagem,
Since things transmit the limits of that visit.

Munmore

Our family name on a row of derelict houses;
The sight of that old plaque suddenly rouses
A passion to know more of the past.

Leaning on the warm bonnet of his car,
A Wexford farmer told me it wasn't far,
Just before Oylgate, off the Enniscorthy road.

Map reading to near the point, I stopped,
Pushed open a cottage gate, propped
By the branch of a tree, and asked the way.

Two Wexford women, gnarled and kindly,
Answered slowly, their faces friendly –
I'd find Munmore beyond the cottage on the right.

The gate posts were there, the drive inviting,
On the left a line of stone-built stabling
And the empty place where the house had stood.

Rooks in the distance, a dog barking through thin air;
Quiet in all these fields and peace where
My family once had lived for generations.

An old trap in the carriage-house; rafters sound;
Balancing dormer windows look on an inner and outer yard,
The remains of a corbelled wall, dressed stones upon the
    ground.

Nothing left, then, to link with any precise sense –
But this past allows imagination's change of tense,
A dreaming back to suit the present mood.

Make castles in Spain, let carriages arrive, come up the drive
To buildings illumined by imagination's inner light, alive
With exuberant sounds of ancestral feasting,

Though underneath these scattered stones, now made so
  trim,
Bleak coldness briefly warmed by self-indulgent whim,
Lie, bone upon bone, bodies of the dispossessed.

Atlantis

Everyone carries some Atlantis sunk deep
In the subconscious, no ripple on the surface
Betrays it to a searching satellite's bleep,
Only deliberate diving, submersing the self,
Reaches weathered contours on ocean shelf.

Once reached, a searchlight in the mind
Pierces the oozy dark, explores those contours,
Mapping out each mathematic parameter,
Constant yet variable, excited to find,
Making wide-ranging self-indulgent detours,
Mount Leinster's every fold and crease,
Then, dangerously speeding up the pulsimeter,
Recognises exactly what was being sought:
A northern boundary stream, old hawthorn trees,
The transformation a bulldozer had wrought:
Beams, hinges, plaster, stones, shattered slates,
Shapeless rubble, remnants of broken gates:
All heaped together. The oxygen runs low,
Light fails to probe the murk, time to follow
Those safety lines back to full consciousness.

Way below the surface, swelling now with waves,
Atlantis lay, a mere sandtable, quite lifeless,
With frozen artefacts the landscape's graves;
From them the conscious mind must build afresh.
Back horses into carriage shafts, bring bran,
Let lusty cockerels crow, set men to thresh
And girls to milk and churn, bid herdsman
Bring fat beasts to market. Fill up the place
And start it into motion.

The next dive down
Finds this strange change: a woman gathering simples,
The mistress in her garden, bonnetted, long gown,
Basket on her arm, thinking, perhaps, of pimples,
Spring electuaries that were efficacious. Marigold
And pulsatilla she picks, euphrasia she crops,
Basing her knowledge on remedies tested and old,

As old as Lady Bountiful's fine hartshorn drops.
In this dead landscape she moves serenely into sight,
Vanishes gently again, into subconscious night.
Her existence has no documentary evidence,
Yet obviously she lived, tended her household,
Cared for the health of others, wanted me to sense
Life's continuity, neither written down nor told,
Briefly offered herself as a distilled essence
Fearing visitors to Atlantis could be blindfold.

New Ross

Thoughts can run on a family tree
Of ancestors long wrapped up in lead.
In Saint Mary's Abbey all are aligned
Beside grey walls. A blazing rose
Surmounts a grave; stone's lettering shows
A bride of but two days is there confined.
She lies in peace. Being of exile-kind
She lived her moth-like love abroad
Till Wexford drew her back with cord
Invisible, with gentlest pressure tied,
Anchored her here by Barrow's side.

South of White Mountain magnetism's stored
In the high-hedged rolling barley country
Where heavy-bodied men their whiskey poured
From gallon jars, drank nights and land away
Till Munmore's seventh son turned runaway,
Became the manager of some defunct distillery
(Although he couldn't stand the smell of drink),
Settled in Dublin, made his own glasses clink,
Called his house Munmore since his prosperity
Enabled him to recreate loved boundaries.

An unwilling exile, three generations on,
I need that space, that heady sea, that river air,
Resounding Wexford names that easily compare
In grace with those of French or Spanish towns:
Monamolin, Camolin, Duffcarrig, Roney Rock,
Townlands my family tilled, deep browns,
Soft greens, large cattle, thick cream in crock,
Home-cured bacon hanging in kitchens' smoke,
Great bulls — one raced the Wexford coach
With drunken rider till his harness broke.

These images impinge. The magnet writes the book
Within my inner mind, makes me imagine I look
At all the objects my family must have loved:
Thatched roofs, whitewashed walls, hawthorn hedges –
Pastoral scenes; Saint Mary's stalls; thick sedges

19

By the two rivers; and by the sea the bent.

What's dramatic? Simply generations and seasons lent
To those who took a long lease on the time they spent
Working here, hearty neighbourly people, enjoying life.
Some parsons, lawyers and doctors in the making
Came to Dublin from these fat fruitful farms
And left the demanding land. Others sailed far,
Down Barrow's or Slaney's tide from the grey quayside,
Daringly on the Atlantic run, to learn their trade:
How to distinguish Virginia leaf, how to grade
At auctions bales for the barques to haul back home.
Their sanguine Norman blondness roused no alarm: no bar
To their returning racily but those of wild wind and sea;
All these arriving ships but stirred the neighbours' curiosity.

Much of their cargo was smuggled upstream,
Excisemen, most likely, wrapped in dream,
Or, still more likely, soaked in bounteous liquor
That celebrated the young men's safe homecoming
To the welcoming grey house, so thankfully humming
With claret, Cork whiskey and the good local beer.
Muffled oars brought the barque *Eleanor* well clear
Of New Ross quay. Donkey cars took half her load
Of leaf, and downstream that black ship slid back;
In the bright morning there'd be no trace, no track
Of donkey's hoof to be discerned. The boss showed
Great generosity, the hospitality his house owed
To the gaugers and tide waiters. Drinking and dance
Died out at dawn, and they had seen nothing –
Glasses in candlelight, yes, sparkles in various eyes,
But rubbing their own, bloodshot, sleepy at sunrise
They heard nothing either, for though near and far
That leaf from each donkey car had spread
No word was said.

                We lived among friends,
Successfully peaceful, dodged all violent ends
In New Ross, where that girl came back to lie
Wrapped up in the peace the wild rose lends.

20

Dreams in Ballask

My dream is of the curving bay,
the yellow strand, the jutting pier,
the sunny warmth of this Wexford day,
the clarity that brings the Tuskar near.

Beyond the Norman castle's stones
lies Churchtown, its forgotten graveyard
grassing over those ancestors' sturdy bones
who'd found their peace in working hard,
farming these lands, fishing, no doubt,
enjoying the air that made it clear
that they were right to have got out,
out of Wales, out of Normandy, before
relaxing here, putting down their roots,
once wives had firmly said 'no more'
to talk of greener fields and richer fruits.

Their dreams were of the curving bay,
with black ships fretting at the jutting pier,
but the sunny warmth of the Wexford day
diverted dreams to the peace that they found here.

This then was their reality, to settle,
graze cattle, estimate their worth with clarity.
Time for me to flatten graveyard's nettles,
peer at tombstones, then take up my own reality.

Images

By the sand at the Barnawheel strand
a fortified house, ruined sheds spanned
by barrel vaulting roofs, aged brick
between the massive stones, thick
walls enfolding an empty past.
Wind through the doors' blank space,
wind on the Norman tower's top,
rugged, like that pushful race
who landed here, thought they'd stop,
let others leapfrog on to build
elsewhere, while they, their passion stilled,
settled into this soil they tilled,
more Irish with every rotated crop.

Carraigseskin

Not an immodest house, Carraigseskin,
For all its tall, three-storied elegance;
It achieves balance without and within,
A rhythmic poise. Banisters subtly curve
Their upward way matched by the swerve
Of plasterwork, all modulated so neatly
The onlooker joins an architectural dance.
Medallions match cornices, the caprices
Of Italian journeymen blending sweetly
With Georgian proportions, mantel pieces
Standing their cool marble guard round grates,
Iron bars blending in the general design,
Mahogany doors echoed in the windows' line,
Though their present state articulates
A very common agricultural policy.

Old corrugated iron excludes the light;
Bales of hay, tight-packed in any vacancy,
Tumble into lobbies, intrude their presence
Upon the past. No one has tidied away
The debris: old photographs give the essence
Of Victorian ease, paintings have more to say
About earlier families posed against their fields,
The house in the background a sign of success.

Now, a mere shell for what the land yields,
It stands an empty symbol of excess
'Since its builder and all later inheritors
Believed in more than the past or present,
Were just house-proud, house-bound servitors
Handing on the house as a commitment
Into an indefinite, ever so ongoing future.

A broken rocking horse, wash-hand stands,
Worn carpets, old shoes all lie at random,
Tired flotsam making no insistent demands,
Emphasising the size of the house, the freedom
Its spaciousness gave. The last son's bungalow
Squats down the drive, brand-new, and system-built;

23

He enjoys it; his freedom was not to follow
Archetypal patterns; he lives, luckily, without guilt.

Their Talk

A major problem this, discovering how they spoke.
What did they wear? How did they occupy their days?
How did they spend their nights? These problems others raise,
Not least what dreams went up their chimney smoke?

Some precise details can easily be amassed:
The cost of mail, where the mail coaches stopped,
Or when the demand for whiskey dropped;
How long their boots and shoes would last.

Such trivial things can bring them closer;
One weighs up this and parcels out that,
Then ranks them on shelves, a country grocer,
Or a milliner measuring Millicent's hat.

Slowly and surely the shop's stock fills
With sacks of statistics, ramifying family trees,
Some items put beneath the counter, wills
And broken hearts and greedy lawyers' fees.

There's snuff or madeira to take in company
That talks of the tobacco trade. This conjures up
More elegant talk when they bite and sup
By candlelight reflected in the mahogany.

Silver the service, but how silvery the speech?
Did they talk politics, view Ireland's bloody heart,
Or plan their picnics on the strand at Ballinoulart,
Or discuss how well their new rector could preach?

Over port what solemn views did they articulate,
These crusty country gentlemen, building bridges,
Repairing fences, some even levelling ridges,
Their well-meant efforts always, perhaps, too late?

An unreal time – two years to ninety-eight
When their easy-going world vanished forever;
And talk took on the urgency of fever,
Their rural peace shattered apart by hate.

Who Fears to Speak of Ninety-Eight?

Enniscorthy – where the Slaney flows
And pale blue buildings pose
Serenely along the river's banks,
And above, in serried ranks,
Grey slated roofs look down;
Higher still the church and castle
Together there symbolically nestle –
You'd think it just a sleepy place
Where peace alone dictates the pace.

Beneath these sleeping roofs, within these walls
Nightmares echo silently, shaken from sleep
When the stark sunlight's searchlight falls
On to dark memories that the old buildings keep
Secret still from strangers: interior knowledge,
Of naked hate, of frenzied fear: pike's edge,
Sword's point, bullet's blast.

                    None here prepare
Rehearsals for a second run, still less unbare
The gruesome acts, the brutal weapons striking home.
Better leave ghosts in peace where each has met his doom,
Invisible now in the cold translucent summer air:
See only the living present within each Enniscorthy room.
None fears, none needs to speak in air which could tear
Old shutters down, stir up those corpses lying everywhere.

Cornwallis's Charity

Reading those faded papers put me in a stir.
Though ill-written their messages ran, brutally clear,
Through informers' letters filed by Major Henry Sirr,
Town Major of Dublin, payer-out of the blood money.

Among them are reports, and one of a court martial
Promptly put the problem of how event and sentence
Related. Cornwallis overrode the verdict, impartial
Hand firmly commuting hanging for a proven offence
To transportation. Judgments and the evidence
After so many years often appear not to fit,
Though this could be true of court reports today.
Why search that faded ink for coloured pilatical truth?
Written reports cannot convey speech, often uncouth,
Confused, stumbling, perhaps reluctant to betray;
The quill records names, a few facts, enought to acquit,
Surprisingly, someone whose involvement seemed explicit.

Cornwallis had no faith in any Irish magistrate.
No punishment was to be inflicted outside courts-martial,
Their judgments must be confirmed by a general –
This he wrote to General Stewart in June to moderate
What he called in July, despairingly, the Irish system of blood.
He had no great faith in courts-martial in any case,
None, obviously, in the one acquitting the yeoman Wollaghan,
Deliberate killer of a pardoned rebel: so to purchase
Confidence in conciliation he put those officers under ban
From ever sitting in judgment again, and the yeoman
He dismissed – for that was all he could do to abase,
To humiliate Lord Enniskillen and the other officers.

Cornwallis was not popular with Sirr's intelligencers –
Nor with their masters, members of the Irish ex-cabinet;
Pitt's policy of Union with Emancipation they overset;
But Cornwallis carried out that Union: believing in duty,
He obeyed orders, despising and hating himself every hour
For engaging, as he succinctly put it, in such dirty work.

ESTABLISHMENT

Final Selection Board

Through the window, sun on Corinthian pilaster,
Architrave reflected in the window beside.
Not a single thing to make the heart beat faster;
Milk chocolate walls, the candidate inside
The circle of the lights centring upon a table,
Glossy laminated wood and shining Swedish glass.
Intelligent civil servants decide if the man is able.

Behind, curved leather screen, fit nest for milliner's lass;
Though no revealing undergarments hang from its top:
Cooing here is done by pigeons, outsiders, who decorate
The gutters, whiten pilasters' stone, and flop
Lazily into Whitehall's sooty air, circle there
And demonstrate their final placings at the top.

Traveller's Tale

'Never go back,' the ambassador said,
'I've never gone back, and I'll soon be dead.'
An impressive remark, so it seemed to me,
And, after all, he *had* climbed the tree.
But then, I wondered, how far could he see?

Could he look back on the way he'd come
Or was he afraid of becoming glum
At things he'd missed or lost on the way,
And didn't look back since he'd gone astray?
This was the kind of thing I meant to say.

But I acquiesced, in most amiable mood,
For, damn it all, I was eating his food.
But I thought to myself, I'd like to go back
For I've really enjoyed all the track
And I thanked my God I'm no Whitehall hack.

At Cambridge

After tea, at the drowsy hour of four,
I took a conversational stroll
With an ex-colonial governor,
Who brooded darkly on proconsular life;
Those black countries he had bravely started
On their bankrupt way to civil strife:
Stiff as a ramrod each time he turned
Right angles in that peaceful quad,
Thoughts marching like a drilling squad,
Machine gun fusillades he farted.
'There's nothing,' he exploded, 'to be learned
Within the confines of a Cambridge quad.'

PLACES

Port River

Monotonous mangrove swamps,
Thumping engine, her wash rippling,
Petersen phlegmatic on the bridge,
Sally Wester tethered to the ramps,
Beneath mackerel clouds' stippling
Mount Lofty and the long blue ridge
Sealing off the dusty baking plain,
Once dubbed 'Greyhound of the Gulf',
The *Karatta* heads to the sea again.
Like Bede's potent image of the sparrow,
Life flits through the hall of time.

Ebb and Flow
(FOR BRIAN ELLIOTT)

Can memories be out of date?
A half-door open; a sandhill;
A sparkling sea: the ebb and rise
Of foaming waves that firmly fill
Electric air at Surfers' Paradise,
Apt background for birds' song
Now drowned in hi-fi from the high rise.

What of the translucent water slapping
Against a jetty in Second Valley?
Could memories be over-lapping?
Like a spring tide I dilly and dally
On the turn, still apparently here,
Now at a high level of recollection
Remembering how in that paradisial cool
Emptiness, bored by beauty, I planned to escape,
Ironically bored by shimmering civilisation:
Close, too close, that planned city scape.
Conflicting dream of living there an isolated pool
Whilst other memories recede with the ebb.

Time's tideless in another thought,
The timeless weeks at Rocky Point:
Shags flapping, pelicans belching,
Undergrowth alive with song,
Crackling dryness, a rustling goanna;
A vast outpouring of energy
Bursting into the air, a symphony
Of urgent life made for the strong
To accept: no idea of 'ought'
Or 'ought not', time in joint,
No mud, no squelching:
Crystal clarity etched deep;
Pure colour, a woman's red bandana,
White tree trunks, black rocks steep
Against limitless azure sky.

Second Valley

Second Valley with sharp and clearcut rocks;
The dirt road leading to the sea;
Eucalyptus, sagebrush and teatree;
A wooden shack with weathered timbers.
The stink of dead wallaby mocks
These aromatic breezes. Wild birds singing;
Blue-greys, sad greens and umbers;
Fence rails and everywhere the wire
Rusted, barbed, twisted and clinging.
A land torn greedily, by fire, scoured,
Parcelled out for sheep, by stump-jumping
Ploughed into semblance of European earth.
This emptiness is haunting; yet no ghosts are here.
Ravaged earth disdains men's mirth,
Their sorrow, too, women's hope and fear.
No peace was made at all; no treaty signed
After long inhabiting, no fields refined
By ceaseless care, no hallowing of earth
Through centuries of marriage; but a rape,
Barrenness: revengeful echoes of outrage
Committed run through the land's monotonous shape;
The bush confines its captors now, within its cage.

Dealer

In the bargaining the bloodshot-eyed Yoruba
Laughs deeply at an impossible price;
Turning away folds the cloth ceremonially;
And I laugh and walk away in my turn.

Next day comes a new stage in the business,
And I hesitate, look thoughtful,
Work out the value of naira . . .
Secretly both know the sale is effected,
So he goes down and I come up
And both of us laugh together.

Next day the notes appear, the cloth is wrapped up;
A final flurry till the bargain's clinched,
Then goodbye until next year.

He also carves thornwood figures
Roughly, effectively and profitably
In the mornings, with apprentices
Learning his craft, become a trade
To capture the tourists' mantel pieces
With synthetic folk art mass-produced
Still containing faint echoes
Of a slower, finer past.

Push for Go

Past swamps of primeval mystery
Men pole laden boats through mist,
A woman washes white clothes
In muddied gamboge water by a bridge.
Broader waters reflect the sky
In blue and white translucency;
Tall trees stand proud of the forest;
Scarlet flowers overflow green growth;
Wrecked cars and trucks are covered
By a creeping carpet, lush foliage
Insinuating the bloody rusted metal
Heaved to the side, out of the tide
Of violent traffic, mammy-wagons
Crammed, lorries overladen, and
Provincial governor's cavalcade of cars –
Blue lights blaring horns blazing out,
Police Peugeots, Mercedes for his Mightiness,
Volvos for the vulgar hangers-on;
A final Peugeot ends the conquering column
Racing to destination of do-good speech:
'Nearly two million barrels last month' –
And many gallons from them burnt by each
Of these cars of the people's pushful people.
But the road remains lined with women
Carrying yams on their heads to market;
Small fires burn before mud houses;
And simple life by this savage road goes on . . .

Onitsha Market

Black goats and kids
(short, plump, frisky)
Clamber contentedly
Over piles of refuse;
Beside them children
Conserve their dignity.
Suburban ladies talk
(Huge headdresses white,
Blue and green robes)
Of their gentlemen friends
Bent in government.
Laughter erupts then;
The market their stage,
They show wealthy market women
Money is not everything,
But enough to bargain with,
To buy exuberant enamel bowls,
Flower-patterned, legend-embellished,
Cheap (lurid but not nasty),
Their outrageous colours echoing
The shouting primaries of the street.

Accra

Tonight we are going to dinner
At some Lebanese dive.
What hope of getting thinner –
We don't walk, we drive!

The Pool

Clouds in Ibadan pile
into continents
While here the pool,
green lagoon,
holds thirteen heads
of screaming, bobbing
children, frog-like;
their elders
round the edge
toad-slump in shade,
in Sunday sloth.

Eldred's Garden

Sleeping Freetown lies in softening haze beneath me;
Beethoven's insistent chords fill up the house:
That cadenced order. Breeze stirs an orange tree;
Some bird's liquid scales fill in the vacant air
That dozes down between this garden and the coast
Where white clouds tower above rain's plumbago layer
Edging in across the sea. Western music tiptoes
To a stop and small birds tune their Sunday choir.

September, Leeds

Three men on stooks, their clothes a faded blue
Sat talking and laughing. Nothing new.
Breughel liked such scenes so casually grouped
In the soft autumn sky. But twine is looped
By binders now, not human hands. The beat
Of combines drifts from nearby fields;
And tractors drone on in September's heat;
And still this good earth smiles and yields
Our winter's food, though we now seem freed
From season's bounty or the winter's need
By marketing, packaging, chemical tricks
Making us forget the need for ricks
Or stooks or men in faded blue
Cracking their jokes from one to two
In their small corner of reality.

Leeds to London

Shining light on the platforms,
Long dark chimneys pointing high,
Orange flame suddenly deforms
The greyness of this winter sky,
Showing it up for its gloom
Intending a note of fierceness
(Redhead typist entering a room
Of balding men in solemn congress).
It indicates the air of doom
Of this ugly man-made mess;
And yet the canal has beauty,
Placid reflections mirror the sky;
Despite its untidy squalidity
It purifies murk that's smoky,
Gives it the sanction of light
Which multiplies the fraction,
Adds natural beauty to the scene,
Supplies a kind of attraction
Through which green grass is seen
Along a towpath's labefaction
Where horses formerly have been,
Dragging man's work, a patient action,
Through a nineteenth century scene.

Saturday Bus

Yorkshire square-rigged dames,
Delicate Pakestani flames
Of colour; West Indian smiles
Wreathe along the bus's miles;
Closepacked, chatting, jerking
As the springs jolt the load
Along the city's inner road,
All bound for bargains lurking
In the city's shopping streets
Where Saturday spree completes
A week of humdrum work –
These women's only perk?
Men, though, will leave the house,
In nearby public house carouse,
Free as the air's apparent space
To act as a superior race.

Deep South

(FOR F. T. PRINCE)

Watching Frank's effortless crawl,
Soldiers bathing came to mind.
Indian light bathing it all
In the reflecting translucency
Of a warm and welcoming sea.
I spent the morning relaxing.

In the afternoon a temple's dark,
Its half-naked priest unwelcoming,
Its architecture shrouded in smoke,
Lacking symmetry, suddenly spoke
To my surprisingly strong monotheism,
So warningly I rushed to clearer air.

Manzamo Cliff

The unreal shapes, the startling black
Of rocks that clasp the bays
Soon sort themselves in memory's track
But later curious questions raise
About the nature of illusion.
Did we really swim off Okinawa,
Or is it just some atomic fusion
Of seascapes in dreams' flowing lava?

Hakkone

The express, the two-coach train, the cable car,
The trees beneath, the sinister sulphur steam,
The lake – and then I wonder where we are,
A sixteenth century galleon out of a dream
Shifts through the mist, diesels heard from afar.

Time Lag

Clock ticks on in Canadian spring;
Cat sleeps on, most cosily enfurled;
Flame flickers on within glass-fronted stove;
Treble glazing shuts off the outer world
(The bare trees threatening sudden growth).
The interior's vacuum-filled; silence falls
In memory's hurry, a snow-storm flurry
Blurring paintings bright on white walls
(Irish trees, farm buildings and a lake).
Past's present here, no spatial break
Though in this midday light I think
That Jeanne's enjoying a six o'clock drink,
(The present continuous beyond horizon's brink).
She's in future time, a gap I'll shrink
Through a jet-lagging transatlantic link.

Atlantic Lullaby

Horizon blends rose into salmon pink
Beneath the slate-blue dark.
Now the day is over,
Plane begins to sink.

Immigration cards are issued,
Soft music is uncanned,
Faces hastily are tissued,
Plane settles down to land.

Flaps down, with rumbling sound
Wheels thrust into the slipstream,
And the plane kisses the ground,
Gently, in a lover's dream.

Lights trace out the runway;
The reverse thrust judders;
Each heart suddenly shudders
With things it cannot say.

Now the void is crossed,
And work will surely keep;
Five long hours are lost,
Now it's time for sleep.

Two Places, Two Races

Louisburg lit by cold winter shafts,
Moonlight filtering through pencil clouds,
Clew Bay's islands mere floating rafts
Sheltered by Croagh Patrick's blackness.
The freezing air grows suddenly thinner;
Turf fire calls, woodcock for dinner.

Another Lewisburg shines in winter air;
Its whitepainted clapboard houses
Sit socially by Susquehanna's side.
Old Pantisocratic dreams float there,
Would-be politicians walk by Bucknell's hill,
Take coffee in faculty club, endlessly talk
Of machinations, deceived and deceivers,
Of ideals (sometimes), yak youthfully on until
Some girl turns the talk to golden retrievers:
Matriarchy making strong sounds and shrill.

Lewisburg, Pennsylvania, purposefully social,
Contrasts with lonely Louisburg in far Mayo,
Where a scanty people find life less crucial;
Unaware they can affect things, come and go
Wrapped in timeless dream, so calm they seem
Cocooned, sealed in by swoon-inducing calm,
Drifting through time in a dark and aged place.

Inland Conference

The professor played out his poststructuralist part
Emphasizing new aspects that we should stress.
But Bagginbun, Boulavogue and Ballinoulart
Murmured their way into my awareness.
Image, symbol, myth, self-destructing fiction
Boomed around, lodged in nodding heads.
But Ireland lost and won, the burning barn,
Tough and crackling images of death's depiction,
Dull blue of steel, yellow surmounting fire's reds,
Consuming stifling women and children in the barn.
Deconstructing the dying traditions, on he lectured.
Those dying on the sea's edge at Bagginbun
Had begun a killing process that ensured
The way the crackling flesh-fed flames would run
Their outrageous politico-social course of cruelty.
He dismissed earlier critics with an easy scorn.
Why, I wondered, should this be happening to me,
This sensing of death, the song of Dermot and the Earl,
The Welsh strumpet throwing hacked captives to the sea,
Her invading Norman lover's death not to be born
Without the instant return, this recycled cruelty.
But the third word slowly began to uncurl,
Unfurl its four syllables of reassuring sound,
Echoing waves curling and furling along the strand,
The empty long reach of it reached by boggy ground
And so, he concluded, such arguments no longer stand.
Bagginbun's bodies disappeared, and Boulavogue's ash,
Ballinoulart's sound turned from myth to fiction,
The sky azure over a place free of human kind.
Unkind, he ended, to the applause, the sudden crash
Of hands, each acquiescent mind meeting mind.
Seabirds on empty strand offered their benediction.

Nice-Pau Express

Milky sea, two seagulls standing
On its creamy edge, immobile
In sun's rays, intently watching
Dark boat, fisherman trimly agile,
Rowing stern foremost close to shore.
The train sweeps on, past harbours,
Cabin cruisers, speedboats, yachts,
Poised, affluent in plastic colours,
Past villas, palms and Mediterranean pots,
Earthen reds, purple rock and shock
Of mustard car on twisting curve
Where road and railway nearly interlock
Then separate in a sudden swerve,
Train bearing inland. Flat market gardens
Alternate with flats in matchbox blocks;
Frejus; inland the outline hardens,
By wooded hills, while men with mattocks
Hack brown earth beside an ancient mas.
Under the autoroute we go: but yesterday,
In Fokker Friendship, it was an overpass.
From the plane I saw a smoke pillar, blue-grey,
Ten-thousand feet high, and wondered whence
It came, and learn today burning rubbish
Sent that signal up. The plane's divulgence
Of shapes of things, from above, was lavish,
But an eye works better at right angles
To the body's stance, and even a glance
From a train transmits, and disentangles,
In human terms, aspects of ignorance,
Translating them into familiar symbols.

East Neuk

Bird plummets into the sea,
The wave sweeps over the rock,
A seal turns its glistering head,
A Phantom howls overhead.

A tanker lies on the skyline,
A lobster boat chugs along,
The wave surges onto the sand,
A teenager alters the waveband.

A Very light hangs high in the sky,
The Marine Rescue Land Rover starts up,
Coast guards move behind their window,
Where will the yellow helicopter go?

Just Names

Munmore, Zion Road; then Milltown's Elm Grove House;
Agathos, Bird Avenue; rooms in the Rubrics;
Suburban Woodstock Road; handier Museum Street;
Then Groningen's brick in H. W. Mesdagplein;
Hofstede de Grootkade, with the canal boats neat
In their coloured serried ranks across the street;
Belwood Lodge, that idyllic cottage at Milton Bridge;
Buccleuch Place, convenient, cheap and cold;
After, Joslin; the shattering heat at South Road;
And Hutt Street's minute house in vast courtyard;
Next Childers Street, our first house bought and sold;
The Dam House at Monk Fryston with its mists
Creeping over the pond and stream; Park Lane
With Roundhay Park's extensiveness, the twists
And turns of its wooden paths, its artificial lakes;
Wester Moss, Rumbling Bridge, in the parish of Muckhart,
With all its friendliness protected, it's very plain,
By the Ochils' shelter and that of the Cleish Hills;
Now Craighead, by the sea at last, not far from Crail.

CATS

Nyjp's Truth

From the moment she appeared from nowhere,
Not fully grown, highly tense and eccentric,
Nyjp wanted to adopt us, never lost a trick
In the game she played for the highest stakes;
She wasn't content – like the six black cats
And the grey and white one with extra pads
Who had appeared from nowhere, the nomads –
To settle for a regular evening meal from us,
Worth staying on for. They formed new habitats
Behind the wooden garage, underneath the shrubs.
She wanted more. She wanted to live with us,
But for a long time we resisted her appeals
While she resisted our approaches; no rubs,
No attempts to stroke her, no friendly gesture.
She wanted entry on her terms, no misdeals.
But we were tending my mother who was dying
And had no desire to assume responsibility.

Nyjp, however, found this resistance most trying,
Gazed reproachfully through windows nightly,
Became very pregnant, and miaouwed, silently,
Until at last one night she broke our will,
For we – looking at her miserable on the sill –
Said together: 'Open the window; let her in!'
She had obviously planned where they'd be born,
Rushed to the open cupboard in the larder
Where the kittens arrived, eyes wide open.
Later a local policeman told us he'd seen her,
Such an elegant, most recognisable cat indeed,
Thrown from a car on the Ring Road months before –
Which explained her tendency to be awkward,
Her reluctance to be touched, back injured;
After a year, she began to relax, to unwind
With great runs after apples thrown in the orchard,
Leap on to Jeanne's back when she was weeding,
And then daringly, tentatively, not fully assured,
She would settle briefly on Jeanne's lap, succeeding
In her efforts to show that she felt accepted.

Her back improved. In Scotland, with casual air,
She simply stepped off the roof of a shed
Eighteen feet high, accurately intercepted
Tiny, her daughter, with dive bomber's flair.

Now, grown old, she rarely climbs a tree,
Makes a wild rush, scurries leaves madly,
But sleeps more, snores, has lost a sabre tooth.
Yet she who was silent, has learned to speak
In a loud voice, now knows how to purr,
Enjoys a soothing hand, brush smoothing fur,
Demands to sit on Jeanne's knee twice a day
Now early memories, neurotic fears away,
Twists her head round to see Jeanne's face above,
Telling her a cat's truth is reciprocal love.

Our Hunter

When Tiny balances on a fence post
She can watch her world go slowly by,
Sparrows and starlings she chatters at,
But she waits most patiently up on high
(Concentrated essence of hunting cat)
For the grass to mark the passage of a mouse.
Then Tiny leaps up into her swallow dive,
Trots with the victim back towards the house,
Uttering most savagely triumphant sounds
On her return from well tried hunting grounds,
Tossing the mouse, patting it, keeping it alive
To re-enact the dance of hunter and hunted
In a masque written by Christopher Smart,
Though rabbits, caught mysteriously at night,
Are killed more quickly, hunger blunted
After peeling off of skin, rejection of spleen,
Enjoyment of saddle, liver and heart.
Tiny is proud of her skill; she takes delight
In patrolling the perimeter, especially if she's seen,
Her assiduous devotion to duty properly praised.

Cat's Love

If a cat likes you
You are fortunate.
You must win
A cat's love,
If, that is, the cat
Is worth knowing;
There are sloppy cats
Who purr, cavort
Like a naive dog
Striving to please;
A true cat
Will tease
Because
Cats are Irish
And tease
Those they love
Or are ready
To consider
Loving

Me

I can eat a butterfly
And assimilate
its colours
I can play with a mouse
and get bored
when it dies
I can treadle with four legs
if I feel exceptionally
pleased
I can leap over a wall in the dark
sink my teeth in a stoat's neck
Which is dangerous
And only to be accomplished
by radar
speaking of which
you probably realise
I am equipped
For heat-seeking
And I can destroy
Anyone's peace of mind
By sitting in their chair
And having to be
ejected
or left
alone
which is what
I like.

WRITING

L'Infinité

Last night a novel wrote itself
before his eyes. Words of a French girl
tumbled out, explaining to herself
how she had seen the waves curl
gently to the sand, to the feet
of the naked man standing there.

Her words made the events neat
and tidy, neutral like the stare
he gave the sea before he turned
and threw away the cigarette,
surprised to learn that she still burned
in the afterglow of their sudden onset.

Sure she was that she'd conceived
a child, outstretched upon that dune,
sure was he that he'd revived
his failing manhood under that moon
whose light reflected in the drop
of sweat that trickled down her face,
focussed his glance, made him stop
short before her, to feel the space
above them stretching out to sea
and then beyond . . .

              She willed his thought
to sense this reaching to infinity;
this was what her naked body'd sought
instinctively when they'd left the car
and lain upon the sand at Roncelegar.

The story spread throughout the night
as they drove further to the south.
He heard it from her shapely mouth,
he heard how, with increasing fright,
she'd dearly paid for that delight
until the novel reached a crux.

He realised then that he'd been used,
unfairly: mere events in their influx
left the simple story incomplete, confused –
of a married boss, with wife ever so wary
of this naively amorous secretary
who wanted infinity – through complexity
of divorce, remarriage and respectability.

She told of the wife wearing a white dress
When, dark glasses on, she made a weekly visit
To her lawyer lover, who stayed nameless.
So, then, who really was the culprit?

He woke in the morning not knowing
why her long hair lay across his chest,
only guessed why her eyes were glowing,
knew his own part in the story dishonest.

Second Sight

Banal music often penetrates the soul
With an emotive impact that explodes
Inside its recording room, changing the role
Of memory. The sound's beat, its tonal codes,
Are translated into mere triggers of vision.
'If I had a talking picture of yoo-hoo' . . .
Lurches over the darksome summer air
Mixed with the hiss of steam, clanking too
Of the aged roundabout, brazen fun of the fair,
But now I see moths fluttering at the window
Soft mountains of featherbed around me
And moonlight on the gravelled road below,
Insistent tune receding into luminosity.
Less aggressive was a snatch of song
Accordion-pleated, horst-vesselled up
In a puff of spiralling wind, drifting along
The steep pine slopes, sentimental as syrup,
Yet calling up that white ship downslipping
Along the silver strip of the Elbe far below.

Words

Words spill from nowhere,
sort themselves onto the page,
make belief in poetic rage –
furor poeticus – seem fair
enough. Inner forces trigger it
into action, make it grow
into shapes imposed by lines,
rhymes, rhythms and designs,
all that the words can show
of emotion put into shorthand,
cloudy thoughts that are lit,
by shafting rays illuminated,
or like patterns on the strand
left by receding waves, foam
lying lightly, like these words
that shape themselves and flow
across the paper; and then slow,
as they reach a full stop.

DEATH

Coiste Bodhar

It passed me in the village
going fast, a black Volvo estate,
curiously illuminated inside.
I could see the four faces clearly,
orderly blond hair, cold blue eyes;
dinner jackets encasing the men,
low-cut dresses revealing the women.
The couple in front were young,
those behind older, parents perhaps;
all staring fixedly ahead.

At the bridge the road turns,
sharply, to the left. But no brake lights
showed. They went straight on.
I waited, sickened, for the sound
of shattering glass and metal, of screaming;
but there was merely silence,
of that brief, unearthly kind,
that follows a crash.
Their lights moved on, straight and impossible
over the hill, and vanished.
Who were they visiting?

The *Coiste Bodhar* is a ghostly hearse seen in the grounds of certain
Irish houses before a death in the family.

Late Ghost

That poor ghost had to be exorcised after we left.
We'd lived in the house for over fifteen years,
Not knowing that the landlady had been bereft,
That this old man shuffling in his carpet slippers,
Striped nightshirt tucked loosely into his pants,
His braces hanging down, had hanged himself.

No, we didn't know – we were Protestants,
And so nobody told us. But he walked:
My father heard him; my mother saw him,
And asked him if she could help him,
So miserable he seemed, wrapped in gloom,
Shuffling slowly across that upstairs room
Then fading from her sight into the dim night
As he reached the stout bar across the alcove.
Her description, we later heard, was right:
Carpet slippers, nightshirt, braces hanging down.

No one had told us of the haunted house's blight
(Probably why its rent was remarkably cheap)
And my parents were content to let him rove
Within that single room, not using it for sleep
But storage once they knew that he existed.

As a child I never knew of him, but used to creep
Quickly past that door in the dark corridor,
Striking matches on the way. It's strange to me
That he never appeared to my father, who was psychic;
He may have thought my mother would be sympathetic
To his bondage, would help him to break free
From his path of mystery. Exorcism did the trick:
No carpet slippers shuffle in that house; he is no more.
I passed it, forty years on, much emptier than before.

Uninvited Guest in Carlow

I could not speak nor scream
but at the moment of despair
suddenly she let go, drew back
contorted face, stood upright
and walked away. I lay there
floating, sea of sweat beneath my back,
greedy for air, my body slack.
When I could move, the thick black
air parted, and I crossed the floor,
drew the curtains, saw the night
lying on the garden, a moon
emerging from thick cloud.
Quiet enveloped the old house.
Then I dressed, sat in a chair,
waited for dawn. When day's fingers
reached into the room, with great care
I opened the door by which she'd left –
a wardrobe, my raincoat hanging there,
no more. No nun's habit, nothing at all
of her, who'd tried to strangle me.
Was it just dream, that swoon
on the edge of death? Mirror showed
livid bruise marks on my throat.

Come and Go

This comes as a sudden jolt –
Enough shoes are here arrayed;
I may not need another suit;
This may be the last bolt
Of Irish tweed I'll get made up,
Something done twice in every decade –
Since I sense the swift pursuit
Arcing down the arching years
Of time who will not stay to sup,
Bringing me – perhaps – among my peers

Friend's Death

Left are our memories of you, tense yet always kind.
Someone told us you left a rational letter behind,
But what is left of the rational in a human mind
That balances, so delicately, on the slippery edge
Of that dark and dread abyss, lonely self-knowledge?

Death

I do not like the idea of death;
The shrivelled limbs, the sagging flesh,
Long gasping fights for breath,
Weariness where nothing's fresh,
Nothing clean, nor clear. All gone
Into decline, running downhill
Fast: no brakes, no bonus coupon
To cash in; only the final bill
To pay. But the living eyes convey
A clue to all there's been,
Only they seem able to say
Something of what you mean;
For the tongue becomes slurred
Within the pursing slipshod lips
And patterns of thought are blurred
As the unheeded saliva drips
Down the withered chin's tracks
And the chain of ideas suddenly slacks
While the frustrating pauses lengthen
Their baffling impediments to speech.
Nothing at all, now, can strengthen
This failing body; nothing can reach
Into the rich treasury of your mind
But glances at those blearing eyes.
Once they glaze over, becoming blind,
None will know how to fathom
Those inmost secrets of your soul
As you escape, breathless, into death.

US

To Jeanne

As a child I never thought I'd sail
The Pacific ocean in a liner, nor own
A house in the south of France;

And as I watched the flying fish
Or the stars from our flat roof
In Lédenon, I didn't believe it:

Was this me, typing a novel on deck
Or, bearded, drinking pastis,
Reading the *Midi Libre*?

The reality, of course, is explicable:
Anything could become a possibility
With you sharing it all with me.

Mother and Child

White square against black glass,
Sunlight piercing darkling cloud,
Two glimmering against dark gloom,
Two only in the world's great crowd.

Climbing up into the greying sky
The Viscount takes me steadily away,
Sunlight still beaming upon you two
Whose brightness irradiates my day.

Lédenon

There's an air of unreality about
the gentle rustling of the fig tree
in the quiet heat of afternoon
when the contented village sleeps
drugged by its dark red wine.

Then silence breaks. There's a shout
to the mule in the shed that tells me
alcoholic ease is over, that soon
the carts will carry high heaps
of weeds from the earth where the vine
demands men's attention, in return
for promise of future fruitfulness,
down on terrain where the burn
of sun's rays will ripen and bless
the villagers' patient labouring.

So long ago since we lived there
in that stark searing southern air
it seems but a classic's dreaming
of Horace, his fig tree and his vine.

Fifty-two

Eight years more, or thirteen?
Has ambition been pushed aside?
It was never large: enough for wife and daughter,
House, car, occasional sun and wine,
Room for friends to stay – and a garden.

True, desire for change as well,
Travel, speed, new faces in new places,
Not to count each penny over-closely,
Have something in the bank, even buy shares,
A place in the country – to get away from it all.

And now I wake in the night and wonder
What will I do with these few years –
Eight or thirteen – which should be different
Though based, no doubt, on the same routine,
Skills (if such they are) and attitudes of mind.

Different, then, in what way?
More serene, possibly leisurely,
Now the targets are hit. More knowledge,
Less memory, perhaps an ability to listen,
Time to write, and an impulse to re-think.

Delights

An overflow of gay excitement,
Such simple joyous things:
My daughter frying bacon,
The kitten playing with string,
Tree peony is blossoming,
Hawk hovers on fluttering wings,
The snarl of a well tuned engine
(Up the road a Scimitar sings),
Words flow on to the paper
Lord, what a pleasure this brings.

Bo's House

Dead rook upon the cobbled hall,
Upstairs two more whose dying fall
Spread soot upon the wooden floor.
These were badges this old house wore
Till their black death gave way to white.
The windows, now open to the southern light,
Reveal the shining sea, birds on each tree
Intensely alive in their singing, ranging free,
Sudden descants gracing their rising flight.
Your coming fills these rooms with life.

Bo's Wedding

The marriage which we celebrate today –
of hearts and bodies joined in unison,
solemnity, high seriousness and fun –
is simple in its setting, and in its way
of ceremony, yet modernly sophisticated;
two religions, one belief, two races now related
in this happy match, where each true mind
can more than a mirror-image find
in the other's complex, rich tradition
of language and art, music and stage –
things acted out or written down on page
to assuage time's many passing pressures
and, more than these, the addition
together of two families' unique features
of living, which, different though they be,
add up to friendship, trust and loyalty.
God bless these two, Felicity and Masaru,
grant them, Mas and Bo, where'er they go
joint life with purpose clear and true.
Here we've gathered friends, in this happy place
Wishing them every happiness and loving grace.

Recovery

To realise Bo's child has come through illness
Is a sudden relief: to see eyes brightening,
Cheeks' colours and contours reflecting no stress,
Gives visible evidence that the spirit's lightening,
No blind hope this but a real lifting of duress.

Love's Truth

Sometimes we got the details wrong
As we grow older,
Mishearing the other, long
To say 'No, colder,
Not hotter'; but 'long'
Is a term too strong
To convey the smile
Which tells how mobile
Such accuracy can be,
How facts don't matter –
Not thin, but fatter –
We share so much, minutiae
Simply can never lie
In the way of overwhelming truth.

WESTER MOSS

Lines of Time

Black and white of winter
splinter against this sky
high with its irradiated light
bright from behind the hill.
Still ribs of trees stark
dark stand upright there
where Roman legions marched
parched in summer's dust,
lust of emperor
for power over Picts
driving them on.

They marched among the Ochil
Hills until they camped
at Ardoch, stamped the straight
road lines across the plain,
again camped, built stone forts,
cohorts, even camp followers
of sorts, holding these posts
on hill tops, watched by
ghosts of men they slew
whose druids clearly knew
the tribes would triumph
in the end, and Rome send
messages of recall.

Their bridge remains in Devon Glen
(this arch their gift to Pictish men)
submerging slowly from passer's view
while contractors crew are marking time
treading lime grey concrete in the dam.
The rising water washes time away;
that vestige of a line to hill fort
vanishes. And what will scour
away our power in times to come
when turbines' hum is lost,
blacked out by outerspacial storm
that sizzles lines from grid,
does more than ever Romans
or Macalpines did
To tidy up the map?

Mood Cærulean

Broad beans, the lilac and holly trees,
Lavender, catmint, blazing peonies,
Yellow pansies, luminous red currants,
Lilies and pinks and, above, blue sky,
Everywhere the exotic aromatic scents.

What need have I, lying here on my back,
Of any radar, seeing I have eyes to track
A 747 up there, seven miles high,
On its rumbling way to the top of the globe?
No need of anything – seeing that I breathe,
Have heard of Dan Chaucer and the astrolabe,
Goonhilly Downs – all that new palaver –
Yet here can see a Flanders-red *papaver*
(Thinking of Latin, Horace and praise of shade)
Lying here dimly hearing jet's engines burning
Appreciating what God (and some men) have
made,
Just faintly conscious of the world's turning
Underneath the moving clouds, the blue rift
Across which in serenest majesty they drift.

Unnatural Planning Permission

A gravel pit threatens this peaceful slope –
poor farming land, it's true, and the farmer too
seems poor, but, if this thirty acre field
is gouged down fifty feet, useless the hope
that 'rehabilitated, reconstituted' land will yield
a pleasure like the present natural view.

Boggy corner whence wild duck rise, where cattle graze
among the tufted weeds; a thicket where roe deer
move swiftly through dappled light; hares laze
in form or lope across the grass, and here
two lapwings dive in menace where cock pheasant
intrudes too near their eggs. It's nature's rant
when curlews cry and crows squawk out at dawn.

This is the natural life that pulses through the land.
Who'd change it for machines extracting sand,
industrial plant growing unnatural upon the hill
with a throbbing diesel stench and grinding mill,
while pounding lorries churn up the mud or dust,
rattle and bang across land once owned by a pawn
removed from the board by the rookish trick
of gravel merchant, of local councillor slick
in the phrases of planning, who with his lust
for gain will change this healthy land to sick,
persuading fools the operation will be quick:
'Five years the period of planning permission;
five acres at a time are worked and five restored.'
If you're fool enough to believe his petition,
this place is planned to die of quick attrition.

Grant the planners some common sense, O Lord;
let them avoid the bribes and do their duty;
let them plan to preserve *some* natural beauty.

Spring's Painting

Daffodils blaze beneath bare chestnut trees,
Glistening starlings preen in gentle breeze,
White lambs graze green fields, and black crows
Stalk brown ploughed land in priestly pose,
Vapour trails roll boldly across blue sky,
Even this pen unfolds words with which I
Record spring's blessings, watch it squeeze
Colours across the scene with lordly ease.

Dog Days

Subtle mists of scent surround us;
Roses abound, mint and thyme
For swallow visitors swooping in,
Their exotic cars filling our yard.
Red Admirals sink without a trace
Gobbled by wagtails with a fond grimace;
The rowan grows apace, and bees begin
Assaulting rich cotoneasters that climb,
Loosely associating with our walls.
Warm western wind clings and falls
About us as joyously we discard
Coats and woollens, the price we pay
Through the rest of the year for living here.

D's Wedding

Claude and Devina standing straight
(No nonsense of her being late),
All moving at a carefully planned rate,
Ian's song bubbling up in melodic joy
And everywhere smiles for girl and boy
In three-litre Bentley, heading their convoy
While the piper leads a walking crowd
Over the wall, the sound loud and proud
Under the trees, no breeze, not a cloud.
And the marquee fills up, from far and near,
Friends enjoying the orthodoxies, the cheer,
The benign witty speeches they want to hear
For this is a very proper country wedding
(Even to later rustic apple-pie unbedding).
On everyone its simple happy lustre shedding.

Advancing Autumn

Autumn is most deceptive. Its speed increases;
The time for painting's gone, firewood's to be cut,
Outdoor lagging to be checked. The light decreases.
Antifreeze is needed, stopcocks must be shut,
And soon the leaves will fill the gutters.
We check the stores in case we're snow-bound,
Sense slow death of growth within the ground.
Thinner air carries the song a blackbird utters,
Aiming his advanced appeal behind our shutters,
While the beat of skeins of geese above soon ceases.
This intense attenuating beauty only teases
With its red reminders, warnings of what's to come.

October

Martins fly in the wood of oak and beech,
Shelter in boughs the sun won't reach,
Zoom up over the stubble in wheeling arcs –
Twittering as if to emulate the larks.

Winter

i Early January

Crows circle in the clear cold air
Fresh filled pools are lying there
Clouds diminish brilliant reflected light
Blazing red sun sinks sliding into night
Below Sight Hill, and the land grows dark.
Bare branched chestnuts stand stiffly stark
Against the icy oyster surface of the sky.

ii Late January

Black mass of pine trees stresses snow's white
Some rose leaves still flutter in the wind
Sheep huddle tight against its biting chill
Seeking shelter below the dyke's low height.

iii Early February

Sun sets in thin blaze behind the hills,
Breughel's snowy, wintry woods between;
Raggedly flying, some late crow fills
Cold sky's striped tent, is seen
Writing its way to the window's edge
While shrivelled leaves along the ledge
Flap sympathetically in the cold keen
Wind that scours the image clean.

iv Late February

In February came a lamb's sudden bleat.
Invisible, in the dark, through sizzling sleet,
It was born at the height of a blizzard
In a night most fierce, savagely hard,
Yet it has survived, looks spry and neat.

Title Index

Index of First Lines